Twelve Short Stories for L

EASY READING
for ESL Students

BOOK 4

by Johnny Bread

CANADIAN LANGUAGE SCHOOL

INTRODUCTION

Easy Reading for ESL Students – Book 4 is a comprehensive reader designed especially for intermediate and advanced students of English as a Second Language. The book was developed and tested by full-time teachers of English.

There are twelve short stories. Each story is designed to engage students in a well-rounded language learning experience. There are comprehension, vocabulary, speaking and writing exercises after each story.

The stories are entertaining and have plot twists and surprise endings. Teachers of English as a Second Language will enjoy using them to engage students on a wide range of topics and interests.

The stories are short (400 – 500 words). Each story and its exercises can be completed in 60 minutes.

You can download a free audio version of the book read by a professional actor. See page 76.

CONTENTS

THE LIFEGUARD

An ordinary man can hold his breath under water for 40 seconds. Jonathan Casey was not an ordinary man. He could hold his breath under water for nine minutes.

When Jonathan was two years old, he fell into a swimming pool. Nobody was watching him. Most children would have drowned – not Jonathan. He was able to get out of the water. That day he learned how to swim.

Swimming had always been an important part of his life. He was on the swimming team at his school, and he had won many competitions. He was in a special diving unit when he was in the navy. Nobody could hold their breath longer than him. His friends called him Frogman.

Jonathan made his living as a lifeguard, and he was one of the best. He retired when he was sixty. Then he started traveling. It was something he had always wanted to do.

One Saturday morning Jonathan was driving on a bridge in Canada. Suddenly the traffic stopped. Jonathan waited and waited. Twenty minutes later Jonathan decided that he had been stuck in traffic too long. He got out of the car.

"Stay in the car, sir," a police officer yelled.

"What's happening, Officer?" Jonathan asked.

"It's an emergency. There's a suicidal woman on the bridge."

Jonathan walked to the side of the bridge and looked. He saw her. A middle aged woman had climbed the railing. She was ready to jump into the water below. Another police officer was talking to her, but she didn't seem to be listening to him.

"Go back to your car," the police officer yelled at Jonathan. And then it happened. The woman let go of the railing and jumped. She seemed to fall for an eternity. Then they heard a big splash, and the woman disappeared under the water.

Jonathan ran to the spot where the woman had jumped and did something unbelievable. He jumped in after her.

Everybody on the bridge looked down. There was no trace of the woman or of Jonathan. One minute passed, three minutes passed, and then six minutes passed. "They are both dead," somebody said. "Nobody can survive under water that long."

Then two heads appeared above the water, and everybody saw Jonathan and the woman. Jonathan had found her and he was pulling her to the river bank.

The woman was in a coma for a month, but she lived. Jonathan became a hero.

"You weren't afraid to die?" a journalist asked Jonathan.

"I was," Jonathan said. "But I just couldn't let her die. I am a lifeguard."

Notes

_____

_____

_____

_____

_____

_____

I. Choose the right answer.

1. Jonathan learned to swim _____.
   - a. when he was five
   - b. when he was three
   - c. when he was two

2. Jonathan was in a special _____.
   - a. swimming unit
   - b. jumping unit
   - c. diving unit

3. Jonathan made his living as _____.
   - a. a swimmer
   - b. a lifeguard
   - c. a traveler

4. After he retired his hobby was _____.
   - a. traveling
   - b. swimming
   - c. diving

5. The woman wanted to kill _____.
   - a. the policeman
   - b. herself
   - c. Jonathan

6. Jonathan was _____.
   - a. afraid to die, but he jumped
   - b. not afraid to jump, but he didn't jump
   - c. not afraid to die, so he jumped

II. Complete the sentences with the words from the box below.

splash	spot	bank	let
eternity	trace	~~stuck~~	coma

1. The cars in front of him were not moving. He was

   _stuck_____ in traffic.

2. The woman _____ go of the railing and jumped into the water below.

3. The woman fell for a long time. It seemed to be an

   _____.

4. When the woman jumped into the water, everybody heard a big _____.

5. Jonathan ran to the _____ where the woman had been standing and jumped.

6. The woman and Jonathan couldn't be seen. There was no _____ of them.

7. Jonathan pulled the woman out of the water. He pulled her to the river _____.

8. The woman was in the hospital for a month. She was in a _____.

III. Choose two words from the box on the previous page and write a short paragraph using them.

_____

_____

_____

_____

IV. Complete the sentences with the expressions from the box below.

hold his breath	diving unit
suicidal woman	ordinary man

1. Jonathan was a special man. He was not an

   _____.

2. Jonathan worked under water. He was in a

   _____.

3. The police officer said, there was a

   _____ on the bridge.

4. Jonathan didn't breathe for six minutes. He could

   _____ for six minutes.

V. Choose two expressions from the box above and write a short paragraph using them.

_____

_____

_____

_____

VI. Answer the question in full sentences.

1. How long can an ordinary man hold his breath?

2. How long could Jonathan hold his breath?

3. How did Jonathan learn to swim?

4. What did Jonathan do in the navy?

5. How did Jonathan make his living?

6. What did he do after he retired?

7. Why was Jonathan stuck in traffic?

8. What did Jonathan do when the woman jumped?

9. Why did he risk his life?

VII. Oral Summary

Retell the story in a few sentences.

VIII. Written Summary

Write a few sentences to summarize the story.

_____

_____

_____

_____

_____

_____

_____

_____

THE DRIVER

Jeff Lowe used to be a professional race car driver. He won many races. He was one of the best.

When Jeff was forty years old, he retired. At the beginning Jeff didn't mind having a lot of free time. Suddenly he could do things he had never been able to do before. For example, he could sleep until ten in the morning. He could also go to the movies, read books and travel. He was able to go out and hang out with his friends every day.

A year later, Jeff was bored. He didn't have to work. He had enough money to live, but he wanted to do something. He had been a driver all his adult life. Driving was the only thing he knew. He decided to become a taxi driver.

At the beginning it was difficult for him. Driving in a big city was very different from driving on a race track, but Jeff got used to it. He got used to dealing with bad drivers. He was very careful and paid attention to everybody on the streets.

Many of his customers praised his driving, but just a handful of them knew they were being driven by the best driver in the city.

Jeff liked his job very much. He met a lot of interesting people. Something interesting was always happening in the city.

"Being a taxi driver is a great job," Jeff thought. "I don't know why taxi drivers are always complaining about things." He was about to find out.

It was around midnight when a man stopped Jeff's taxi. As the man got into the taxi, two other men ran from around the corner and got into the taxi, too. They knew one another. They were criminals.

"Give me all your money!" one of them said. "And do it quickly." The man pulled a knife on Jeff.

Jeff gave him all his money.

"Now drive us to the train station," the man said. Drive fast. We don't want to miss the train."

"Yes, sir," Jeff said. "I will drive fast. You'd better fasten your seatbelts."

The three men will never forget what happened. Jeff drove his taxi as if it were a race car. For a few minutes he became a race car driver again. The man dropped the knife and grabbed his seat. The two others grabbed their seats, too. It was their worst nightmare. The men were frightened and worried about their lives.

When Jeff stopped the taxi, the men didn't move. They were frozen with fear. Jeff called the police. While the police were arresting the men, they all shouted, "He wanted to kill us! He wanted to kill us!"

"You wanted me to drive fast, didn't you?" Jeff said and smiled.

Notes

_____

_____

_____

_____

_____

I. Choose the right answer.

1. Jeff used to be a _____.
   a. criminal
   b. police officer
   c. race car driver

2. When he was forty, he _____.
   a. retired
   b. had an accident
   c. got married

3. Later Jeff became a _____.
   a. criminal
   b. taxi driver
   c. truck driver

4. Jeff was a _____ driver.
   a. careless
   b. careful
   c. bad

5. The man who stopped Jeff _____.
   a. was his friend
   b. was a police officer
   c. was a criminal

6. The men were frightened _____.
   a. because Jeff drove fast
   b. because Jeff had a gun
   c. because Jeff had a knife

II. Complete the sentences with the words from the box below.

grabbed	frightened	dealing	attention
praised	fasten	~~adult~~	handful

1. A fully grown person is called an _adult_____.

2. Jeff encountered many bad drivers, but he got used to _____ with them.

3. Jeff thought about other people a lot. He paid _____ to them.

4. Many people said good things about Jeff. They _____ him.

5. Not many people recognized Jeff. It was just a _____ of them who recognized him.

6. Before you start driving, you have to _____ your seatbelt.

7. The three criminals took a hold of their seats. They _____ them.

8. The men were worried about their lives. They were _____.

III.   Choose two words from the box on the previous
       page and write a short paragraph using them.

_____

_____

_____

_____

IV.   Complete the sentences with the expressions from
      the box below.

hang out	race track
miss the train	about to

1. Jeff went out with his friends. They didn't do much.

    They just wanted to _____.

2. The area for car racing is called a

    _____.

3. Jeff didn't know about taxi drivers' problems, but he was

    _____ find out.

4. The men wanted to get to the train station fast. They

    didn't want to _____.

V.   Choose two expressions from the box above and
      write a short paragraph using these expressions.

_____

_____

_____

_____

VI. Answer the questions in full sentences.

1. What did Jeff use to do for a living?
2. When did he retire?
3. What did he do when he retired?
4. Why did he need a job?
5. What kind of job did he choose and why?
6. How did Jeff like his new job?
7. How did Jeff find out that his job could be difficult?
8. What did the criminals want from Jeff?
9. How did Jeff deal with the criminals?

VII. Oral Summary

Retell the story in a few sentences.

VIII. Written Summary

Write a few sentences to summarize the story.

_____

_____

_____

_____

_____

_____

_____

_____

THE OLD CITY BLUES

Lisa McGee was born in Coldwater, Mississippi. Her parents were not rich, but they were kind and hardworking people.

Lisa's family was big, but the most important person in her life was her grandfather. Lisa loved her grandfather. He was a musician and taught her how to sing and play musical instruments. He had discovered Lisa's talent for music and singing when she was only two years old and thought it would be worth helping her develop her talent. They got together as often as they could. Lisa sang, and her grandfather played the piano or the guitar.

Lisa dreamed that she would sing on the stage one day, and people would applaud her and admire her.

Lisa's grandfather often told Lisa stories. Her favorite story was about an old city somewhere in Europe which her grandfather had once visited.

"The city is so old that it remembers the kings and queens," her grandfather said. "There is a big castle and hundreds of churches. It has beautiful squares and bridges with magnificent statues. There are streets so narrow that two bikes cannot pass each other." Her grandfather had even written a song about the old city, which he and Lisa often sang together. He called it *The Old City Blues*. The song was so beautiful and touching that it brought tears to Lisa's eyes every time they sang it.

Lisa grew up. Her dream didn't come true. She didn't become a singer. She worked in a store and sang only for pleasure. But there was something Lisa wanted to do very much. She wanted to visit the old city her grandfather had told her about. She had been saving money for that purpose.

When Lisa was forty years old, she thought it was about time to go on a trip to Europe. The funny thing was that her grandfather had never told her the name of the city, and she had never asked him. Her grandfather had died years earlier.

Lisa went to a travel agency and described the old city in Europe to an agent.

"Well, almost every major city in Europe fits that description," the agent said.

"OK," Lisa said. "Which of these cities would be the cheapest to visit?"

The agent looked at his computer screen for a long time. At last he said, "Prague."

Lisa went on vacation to Prague for two months. Two months became five years. Today Lisa is still in Prague making her living as a singer in a jazz club. How did she do it? People say it was because of the blues song she sang one night while visiting a jazz club. The song brought tears to people's eyes, and the manager of the club never let her go.

Notes

_____

_____

_____

_____

_____

I. Choose the right answer.

1. Lisa was born in _____, Mississippi.
    - a. Hotwater
    - b. Warmwater
    - c. Coldwater

2. Lisa's parents were _____.
    - a. kind but lazy
    - b. strict and hardworking
    - c. kind and hardworking

3. Lisa's grandfather was a _____.
    - a. musician
    - b. farmer
    - c. travel agent

4. Lisa wanted to become a _____.
    - a. singer
    - b. travel agent
    - c. jazz club manager

5. Lisa's first job was _____.
    - a. on a farm
    - b. at a store
    - c. in a club

6. Lisa chose to go to Prague because _____.
    - a. her grandfather told her to
    - b. it was in the Czech Republic
    - c. it was relatively cheap

II. Complete the sentences with the words from the box below.

pleasure	magnificent	~~blues~~	touching
applaud	develop	narrow	talent

1. The song about the old city was sad and touching. It was a _blues_ song.

2. Lisa had a natural ability to sing and play musical instruments. She had _____.

3. Lisa's grandfather practiced with Lisa a lot. He wanted to _____ her talent.

4. When people are satisfied with an artist's performance, they _____.

5. The statues were very beautiful. They were _____.

6. Some streets were so _____ that two bikes couldn't pass each other.

7. The song was so beautiful that people had tears in their eyes. It was _____.

8. Lisa was not a professional singer. She sang only for her own _____.

III. Choose two words from the box on the previous page and write a short paragraph using them.

_____

_____

_____

_____

IV. Complete the sentences with the expressions from the box below.

brought tears	making her living
got together	funny thing

1. Lisa and her grandfather often _____ and played music.

2. The song was so touching that it _____ to people's eyes.

3. Lisa never asked her grandfather the name of the city. It was a _____.

4. Lisa sings, and she is paid for it. She is _____ as a singer.

V. Choose two expressions from the box above and write a short paragraph using these expressions.

_____

_____

_____

_____

VI.   Answer the questions in full sentences.

1. Where was Lisa born?
2. What were her parents like?
3. Who was the most important person in Lisa's life?
4. What did he teach her?
5. What was Lisa's dream?
6. What was Lisa's favorite story?
7. What did Lisa want to do after her grandfather died?
8. Why did she choose Prague?
9. How did Lisa's life change after she visited Prague?

VII.   Summary

Retell the story in a few sentences.

VIII.   Written Summary

Write a few sentences to summarize the story.

_____

_____

_____

_____

_____

_____

_____

_____

A DIPLOMAT

A luxury car was slowly moving down a street in a big hot city. It was Sunday afternoon, and there weren't many cars on the street. All of a sudden a motorcycle appeared from nowhere, and the rider rode parallel to the car for a few seconds. It was a powerful racing motorcycle. The rider was wearing a black leather suit and a helmet with a black face shield. He drew a gun from a holster strapped to his thigh and smashed one of the car windows.

Two men and two women were sitting in the car. They were wearing nice clothes. The driver stepped on the brake and stopped.

"Give me all your money and jewelry or you die," the motorcycle rider said.

The frightened people in the car gave the rider all the money and jewelry they had.

"Thanks," the rider said. In a few seconds he was riding at a speed of 100 miles per hour. Then he disappeared from view.

The rider was Paolo Sousa. He loved robbing rich people more than anything else. He had been doing this for years. With a motorcycle that could go up to 200 miles per hour and a gun he felt invincible.

Paolo grew up in a poor family. His father and grandfather had taught him to hate rich people, and he did. But Paolo didn't want to live like his father and grandfather. To hate the rich wasn't good enough for him. He wanted to do something more.

Paolo had worked very hard. It took him more than ten years to make enough money to buy a racing motorcycle. After his first robbery Paolo knew that there was nothing else he would rather do than rob the rich while riding his powerful motorcycle.

One day Paolo spotted a shiny black limousine parked in front of a luxury hotel. The driver was apparently waiting for somebody. Paolo watched as an old man in a nice suit got in, and the driver drove away.

"Show time," Paolo said to himself and started the motorcycle. He rode next to the limousine and hit the window with his gun, but this time the window didn't break. He tried again and again – nothing. Then the window opened. Paolo was so surprised that he didn't have time to react. A powerful hand grabbed his gun and pulled him against the car door. Paolo fell off his motorcycle. The car stopped. Paolo was lying on the ground. The old man got out of the car and pointed a gun at Paolo. "You made a mistake you petty thief," the old man said and called the police.

"Who are you?" asked Paolo. He couldn't understand what had happened to him.

"I am a diplomat," the old man said calmly. "Never mess with a diplomat."

Notes

_____

_____

_____

I. Choose the right answer.

1. The robber was _____.

    a. walking down the street
    b. riding a motorcycle
    c. driving a car

2. The robber _____.

    a. broke a car window
    b. crashed into the car
    c. shot out the car tires

3. Paolo grew up in a _____ family.

    a. rich
    b. middle class
    c. poor

4. Paolo enjoyed _____ rich people.

    a. robbing
    b. beating
    c. helping

5. To own a motorcycle Paolo _____.

    a. had to steal it
    b. had to work very hard
    c. had to ask his father to buy him one

6. It was a mistake to _____.

    a. kill a diplomat
    b. become a diplomat
    c. mess with a diplomat

II. Complete the sentences with the words from the box below.

smashed	~~parallel~~	petty	apparently
thigh	leather	invincible	strapped

1. The rider was riding next to the moving car. He was riding _parallel_____ to the car.

2. The rider was wearing a black _____ suit.

3. The part of the leg between the hip and the knee is called the _____.

4. The rider had a holster with a gun in it _____ to his thigh.

5. The rider _____ the window. It broke into pieces.

6. Paolo thought that with his motorcycle and gun he was _____.

7. A driver was sitting in the limousine. He was _____ waiting for somebody.

8. We call somebody who steals small things a _____ thief.

III. Choose two words from the box on the previous page and write a short paragraph using them.

_____

_____

_____

_____

IV. Complete the sentences with the expressions from the box below.

mess with	disappeared from view
all of a sudden	from nowhere

1. Nobody expected it. _____ there was a motorcycle.

2. It appeared _____.

3. The rider robbed the people in the car and

   _____.

4. It's not a good idea to _____ a diplomat.

V. Choose two expressions from the box above and write a short paragraph using them.

_____

_____

_____

_____

_____

VI.   Answer the questions in full sentences.

1. Where did the story happen?

2. What happened at the beginning of the story?

3. Who was the rider?

4. What was Paolo's childhood like?

5. What did his father and grandfather teach him?

6. What did Paolo do later in his life?

7. How did Paolo feel with his motorcycle and gun?

8. What went wrong for Paolo one day?

9. What was Paolo's mistake?

VII.   Oral Summary

Retell the story in a few sentences.

VIII.   Written Summary

Write a few sentences to summarize the story.

_____

_____

_____

_____

_____

_____

_____

_____

_____

A DATE WITH A GHOST

I will never forget that day. It was at the end of October. It was early morning, and I was running along a path in the woods. I didn't see anybody anywhere. I was alone. I enjoyed being alone. I was used to it.

Suddenly a woman appeared from nowhere and started to run behind me. I wouldn't have minded, except she was running too close to me. It made me nervous. I slowed down to let her pass. She slowed down, too. I ran faster to outrun her. She ran faster, too. She was right behind me.

We ran together like this for about twenty minutes. I wanted to stop and ask her what she wanted, but I didn't. I would have looked stupid.

I was in good shape. I had run many marathons. I started to run really fast. I had decided to lose her. She kept up with me for about five minutes. She was apparently in good shape, too. But then she gave up.

I continued running for a while. The woman was nowhere to be seen. I ran out of the woods and sat down on a bench. I was thinking about the woman. It was weird. She was weird. Or was I exaggerating?

Suddenly she walked out of the woods and walked up to me. A tingle of fear ran down my back. Was I frightened of her?

She sat down next to me. "Did I scare you?" she asked smiling.

"No," I said. "Not at all."

"I am sorry," she said. "I don't like running alone. We could run together sometimes. What do you think?"

"I don't know," I said. "I like running alone."

"You might change your mind if we get to know each other," she said. "I'll come to your apartment. I know where you live." She didn't wait for my answer. She got up and ran back into the woods. It was mind boggling.

I went home and told Josh everything. Josh was my roommate. We had been living together since we were in college.

Josh became very serious. He went to his room and brought me a picture printed from the Internet. "Is this her?" he asked.

"Yes," I said. "Who is she?"

"Her name was Savanna Sutherland. She was very clever and pretty. The problem is that she died ten years ago. She was murdered in the woods nearby. You have a date with a ghost."

"You seem to know a lot about her," I said. "How is that?"

Suddenly the door of my room opened, and Savanna Sutherland walked in.

"It's because he's my cousin," she said. "We played a trick on you. Happy Halloween, Brendan." They both started to laugh.

Notes

_____

_____

_____

I. Choose the right answer.

1. Brendan was _____.
   a. climbing a mountain
   b. hiking
   c. running

2. A _____ appeared from nowhere.
   a. wolf
   b. woman
   c. wild boar

3. Brendan felt _____.
   a. happy
   b. angry
   c. nervous

4. The woman _____.
   a. attacked Brendan
   b. suggested a date to Brendan
   c. outran Brendan

5. Josh was Brendan's _____.
   a. roommate
   b. inmate
   c. classmate

6. Savannah was _____.
   a. Josh's cousin
   b. Josh's sister
   c. a ghost

II. **Complete the sentences with the words from the box below.**

roommate	exaggerate	weird	ghost
slowed down	~~except~~	murdered	outrun

1. I didn't mind running with her _except_ she was too close to me.

2. I didn't run as fast as before. I _____.

3. I wanted to get away from her, so I started to run faster. I wanted to _____ her.

4. I thought the woman was very strange. I thought she was _____.

5. Then I thought something was wrong with me. "You _____," I thought.

6. Josh shared an apartment with me. He was my _____.

7. According to Josh the woman was killed. She was _____.

8. Josh said that Savannah Sutherland was dead, and I had spoken to her _____.

III. Choose two words from the box on the previous page and write a short paragraph using them.

_____

_____

_____

_____

IV. Complete the sentences with the expressions from the box below. Use the past tense.

mind boggling	kept up with me
played a trick	tingle of fear

1. The woman ran as fast as I did. She

   _____.

2. I felt excitement mixed with fear. A

   _____ ran down my back.

3. I couldn't believe what the woman said. It was

   _____.

4. The ghost story was not true. Josh and Savannah

   _____ on me.

V. Choose two expressions from the box above and write a short paragraph using these expressions.

_____

_____

_____

_____

VI. Answer the questions in full sentences.

1. What was the man doing at the beginning of the story?
2. Who was he with?
3. What happened?
4. What did the man do?
5. What did the man think about the woman?
6. What did she tell him?
7. How did he feel about it?
8. What did Josh tell him about the woman?
9. What happened in the end?

VII. Oral Summary

Retell the story in a few sentences.

VIII. Written Summary

Write a few sentences to summarize the story.

_____

_____

_____

_____

_____

_____

_____

_____

_____

A HORSE WHISPERER

Daisy lived with her parents in New York City. Since she was a little girl, she had been interested in horses. She was a member of a horse club and rode horses every weekend. Daisy wanted to become a veterinarian and help horses.

When she was fourteen years old, she went to Texas to spend her vacation with her grandfather. He had a ranch where he raised horses. Her grandfather was very happy to see his granddaughter for the first time. Daisy was very happy, too. Her grandfather's ranch was one of the biggest in Texas.

"I'm always very busy," her grandfather said. "You can go and play anywhere on the ranch except that stable. Never go there."

"Why not Grandpa?"

"There is a horse in that stable. He is very dangerous. Last week he attacked a man."

"Horses don't attack people," Daisy said. "Unless something bad happened to them."

Her grandfather smiled. "You seem to know a lot about horses."

"Almost everything," Daisy said proudly. "I have sixty-eight books about horses in my collection. I have read them all."

"The horse was in a car accident," her grandfather said. "A car hit his trailer. He was so scared that he went crazy. I got a veterinarian and even an animal psychologist to come and see him. Nobody could help him. He is still alive because he was one of my favorite horses. But I can't keep him alive for long."

"Can I see him? Daisy asked.

"No, never," her grandfather said. "Do not dare go near him."

"OK," Daisy said.

Daisy couldn't sleep that night. She was thinking about the horse. Suddenly she got up. It was two in the morning. Everybody on the ranch was sleeping. She took her flashlight and a carrot from the kitchen and went to the stable. She opened the stable gate and walked in. She switched on her flashlight. Then she saw him. He was a big black horse. He was looking at her. *Black Devil* somebody had written on his stall.

"Hi," Daisy said quietly. "I see you can't sleep. Something is bothering you. I can't sleep either. Do you want to be my friend?"

The horse watched her with his big black eyes. He didn't move.

Daisy gave him the carrot. Surprisingly he ate it.

Daisy went to see the horse every night. She brought him something to eat, and then she talked to him. Two weeks later she was riding him. Daisy had cured the horse. Her grandfather was proud of her.

A journalist learned about the story and came to see Daisy on the farm.

"What did you tell the horse when you were alone with him?" she asked curiously.

Daisy smiled. "It's my secret," she said.

The story was in the newspaper. *The fourteen-year-old horse whisperer,* the headline said.

I. Choose the right answer.

1. Daisy lived in _____.
   a. Plattsburg, New York
   b. Oswego, New York
   c. New York, New York

2. Daisy was interested in _____.
   a. dogs
   b. horses
   c. cats

3. Daisy wanted to become a _____.
   a. physician
   b. veterinarian
   c. jockey

4. Black Devil went crazy _____.
   a. because he was in a car accident
   b. because he was mistreated
   c. because he got sick

5. Daisy cured Black Devil _____.
   a. using witchcraft
   b. using drugs
   c. by talking to him

6. A journalist called Daisy _____.
   a. the horse whisperer
   b. a witch
   c. a good vet

II. Complete the sentences with the words from the box below.

curiously	cured	stall	flashlight
~~stable~~	proudly	carrot	collection

1. Horses are usually kept in a _stable_____.

2. Daisy knew a lot about horses and talked about it very

   _____.

3. Daisy had a lot of books about horses. It was a nice

   _____.

4. It was dark in the stable, so Daisy used a

   _____.

5. Daisy needed to give the horse something to eat. She

   gave him a _____.

6. An enclosed area in a stable for a horse is called a

   _____.

7. The horse was healthy again. Daisy _____ him.

8. "What did you tell the horse?" the journalist asked

   _____.

III. Choose two words from the box on the previous page and write a short paragraph using them.

_____

_____

_____

_____

IV. Complete the sentences with the expressions from the box below.

seemed to	went crazy
horse whisperer	do not dare

1. Daisy _____ know a lot about horses.

2. After the car accident the horse was not well. He

   _____.

3. Daisy wanted to see the horse, but her grandfather said,

   " _____."

4. An individual who trains wild horses is called a

   _____.

V. Choose two expressions from the box above and write a short paragraph using them.

_____

_____

_____

_____

38

VI. Answer the questions in full sentences.

1. Where did Daisy live?
2. What was she interested in?
3. What did she want to become?
4. Where did Daisy's grandfather live?
5. What did he do for a living?
6. What did he tell Daisy?
7. What was wrong with the horse?
8. How did Daisy cure the horse?
9. What did the journalist call Daisy?

VII. Oral Summary

Retell the story in a few sentences.

VIII. Written Summary

Write a few sentences to summarize the story.

_____

_____

_____

_____

_____

_____

_____

_____

_____

LADY DEER

Sam was lying in bed and staring at the ceiling. It was 3:30 a.m. He couldn't sleep. He had had trouble sleeping lately. Somebody was on his mind again.

Sam looked at his watch. He couldn't take it anymore. He got up and put on his jogging suit. Ten minutes later he was running in the forest. It was dark and Sam was alone. Nobody was crazy enough to run in the forest at night to fight their insomnia.

All of a sudden Sam heard a noise behind him. He stopped and turned around. He saw a big grey hunting dog running towards him. Sam was not normally afraid of dogs, but this one scared him. He was very big. Sam thought about climbing a tree, but it was too late. The dog was too close.

The dog stopped about ten feet from Sam and watched him with his big eyes. Then Sam realized it was not a dog. It was a doe. They stared at each other for a minute. Then Sam moved forward. He had gotten a crazy idea to pet the doe. Now Sam was really near her, but she didn't move. It was unbelievable. Weren't deer supposed to be afraid of people? This one obviously wasn't.

Sam took a few steps and raised his hand to pet the doe. But as he did it, the doe turned around and ran away.

The next day was Friday. Every Friday Sam got together with his friends. He told them about his adventure while they were drinking beer. Of course his friends joked about it. One said he should talk to the ranger about it. The doe might have rabies. The other one said he should talk to a shrink about it. It was not normal to run in the forest at night. Then one of his friends told him about an old woman living in the forest. She knew everything about the forest. She might be a witch. He could talk to her.

Sam decided to find the old woman. He thought it might be fun to talk to her. So the next day he went on a hike to look for her.

After a five-hour search, he found her deep in the forest. She was picking some plants. John told her about the doe.

"Of course I know her," she said. I call her Lady Deer. She is not an ordinary doe. I think she is an enchanted lady looking for her lost love. She is only attracted to people that are in love. She often follows them in the forest."

She stopped talking and looked at Sam. "Are you in love yourself?" she asked.

Sam laughed. "Me? No. That's ridiculous."

"Is it?" the old woman said. "Because Lady Deer follows only those who are in love. She can feel it. She never makes a mistake."

Sam's face turned red. He stopped laughing. "Do you have something for insomnia?" he asked.

"Not for *your* insomnia," she said. "You will have to deal with it on your own."

"I will," Sam said. "Thank you for telling me the truth about myself. Now I know what to do. I will ask her out. She might say yes or she might say no, but I will finally know."

"Don't thank me. Thank Lady Deer."

Notes

_____

_____

I. Choose the right answer.

1. Sam couldn't sleep because _____.
   a. he had eaten too much
   b. he was thinking about somebody
   c. he was thinking about his work

2. Sam tried to fight his insomnia _____.
   a. by taking sleeping pills
   b. by drinking alcohol
   c. by running

3. Sam thought he was being _____.
   a. followed by a boar
   b. followed by a bear
   c. followed by a dog

4. Sam wanted to _____ the doe.
   a. pet
   b. chase away
   c. pat

5. Sam decided to see _____.
   a. the ranger
   b. the old woman
   c. a shrink

6. The old lady told Sam to _____.
   a. help himself
   b. drink her special tea
   c. eat special berries

II. **Complete the sentences with the words from the box below.**

shrink	doe	~~insomnia~~	enchanted
attracted	ridiculous	rabies	pet

1. Sam wasn't able to sleep at night. He suffered from
   _insomnia_____ .

2. A female deer is called a _____ .

3. Sam wanted to gently touch the doe. He wanted to
   _____ her.

4. If you are bitten by an infected animal, you could get a
   virus called _____ .

5. A psychiatrist is sometimes humorously called a
   _____ .

6. The old lady thought there was magic, and the doe was
   an _____ lady.

7. Lady Deer followed only people in love. She was
   _____ to them.

8. Sam thought there was no way he could fall in love. He
   said it was _____ .

III. Choose two words from the box on the previous page and write a short paragraph using them.

_____

_____

_____

_____

IV. Complete the sentences with the expressions from the box below.

couldn't take it	on his mind
all of a sudden	supposed to be

1. Sam often thought about somebody. She was often

_____.

2. Sam couldn't sleep. He was very upset. He

_____ anymore.

3. Sam didn't expect an animal to follow him. It happened

_____.

4. Deer are _____ afraid of people, and

they usually are.

V. Choose two expressions from the box above and write a short paragraph using them.

_____

_____

_____

_____

44

VI. Answer the questions in full sentences.

1. What was Sam's problem?
2. Why wasn't he able to sleep?
3. How did he try to fight his insomnia?
4. What happened to him in the forest?
5. Why was Sam surprised?
6. What did his friends tell him?
7. What did Sam decide to do?
8. What did the old woman tell him?
9. What was Sam's final decision?

VII. Oral Summary

Retell the story in a few sentences.

VIII. Written Summary

Write a few sentences to summarize the story.

_____

_____

_____

_____

_____

_____

_____

_____

_____

_____

THE MOUSE

Rolf Crust was running in the woods. He had been running a lot lately. He had been training for the Boston Marathon. This year he wanted to finish among the first one hundred participants.

It was about five in the morning. He was always alone in the woods so early but not today. He saw somebody near the edge of a cliff. It was a woman, and she was sitting in a wheelchair. Very strange – how had she gotten there in a wheelchair? But Rolf didn't have the time to think about it.

"Oh my God!" Rolf cried. The woman was rolling towards the edge of the cliff. She was about to fall 100 feet. She was about to die.

Rolf ran towards the woman and had to throw himself to the ground in order to grab one of the wheels of her wheelchair. He saved her life just in the nick of time.

The woman turned around. She didn't seem to be grateful. There was anger in her eyes. "You shouldn't have saved me," she said. "I wanted to die. But…" She had tears in her eyes. "Thank you, anyway."

"What is your name?" Rolf asked.

"Ann," she said. "But nobody calls me that. You should have seen me before my accident. I used to go rock climbing. My friends called me Cat because I could climb anything. Then one day two years ago, I fell, and I have been in a wheelchair since. It's not a life. I don't want to live anymore."

Rolf looked at the woman closely. "I'm Rolf," he said. "But nobody calls me that either. And I came here for a reason. I think it was fate that brought us together this morning."

"What do they call you?" she asked.

"Mouse," he said smiling.

She smiled a little. "You're a liar."

"No, I am not. It goes back to my childhood. When I was a little boy, I was small and skinny. I was often bullied by my classmates. Once they went after me, and I managed to crawl through a hole in the fence. Nobody else was able to do that. They started to call me Mouse after that."

She had a big smile on her face now. "Are you saying that Mouse has saved Cat?"

"That's exactly what I am saying," Rolf said. "And not just that. I'm your guardian angel."

Rolf and Ann started seeing each other often. They became friends, and their friendship grew into something more. Rolf helped Ann with her exercises and her recovery whenever he could. They both suddenly had new energy to live their lives. Rolf finished third in the Boston Marathon, and Ann slowly started to recover from her injury. She was getting better and better.

One day when they met, Ann wasn't in her wheelchair. She was beaming with joy. Suddenly Rolf became sad. "I can see you have recovered," he said. "You won't need me anymore."

"What are you talking about, Mousie?" Ann said. "From the beginning of time Cat and Mouse have belonged together. They can never be separated."

Notes

_____

_____

I. Choose the right answer.

1. Rolf was _____.
   - a. cutting wood
   - b. running
   - c. picking mushrooms

2. Rolf wanted to finish _____.
   - a. the marathon
   - b. at least in the top 100 in the marathon
   - c. 100th in the marathon

3. The woman was _____.
   - a. in a wheelchair
   - b. pushing a wheelchair
   - c. getting rid of a wheelchair

4. Cat was the woman's _____.
   - a. real name
   - b. pet
   - c. nickname

5. Rolf was called Mouse _____.
   - a. because he didn't like cats
   - b. because he liked mice
   - c. because he had escaped through a hole

6. They couldn't be separated _____.
   - a. because they loved each other
   - b. because they were Cat and Mouse
   - c. because Rolf saved Ann's life

II. Complete the sentences with the words from the box below.

closely	~~participants~~	wheelchair	fate
beaming	recover	skinny	tears

1. Thirty thousand people ran the marathon. There were 30,000 _participants_ .

2. The woman was sitting in a special chair for disabled people. She was in a _____.

3. Rolf looked at the woman with great interest. He looked at her _____.

4. Rolf believed he didn't spot the woman by accident. He believed it was _____.

5. The woman was crying. She had _____ in her eyes.

6. When Rolf was a little boy, he used to be very thin. He used to be _____.

7. Ann was getting better and better every day. She started to _____.

8. Ann was very happy. She had a big smile on her face. She was _____ with joy.

III. Choose two words from the box on the previous page and write a short paragraph using them.

_____

_____

_____

_____

IV. Complete the sentences with the expressions from the box below.

in the nick of time	seem to be
about to fall	managed to crawl

1. The woman was going to fall in a few seconds. She was

   _____.

2. She had an angry expression on her face. She didn't

   _____ grateful.

3. Rolf saved the woman at the last second. He saved her

   just _____.

4. Rolf was able to disappear through a hole. He

   _____ through it.

V. Choose two expressions from the box above and write a short paragraph using them.

_____

_____

_____

_____

VI. Answer the questions in full sentences.

1. What was Rolf doing in the woods?
2. What did he see at the edge of a cliff?
3. What was the woman's intention?
4. What did Rolf do?
5. Why was the woman called Cat?
6. Why was Rolf called Mouse?
7. What happened after Rolf saved Ann's life?
8. Why did Rolf suddenly become sad?
9. Why couldn't Ann and Rolf be separated?

VII. Oral Summary

Retell the story in a few sentences.

VIII. Written Summary

Write a few sentences to summarize the story.

_____

_____

_____

_____

_____

_____

_____

_____

_____

THE RED JEEP

Since he was a little boy Jarrett had loved playing with cars. He had a huge collection of toy cars at home. His favorite toy was a red Jeep. He spent many hours outside playing with the Jeep. It was his favorite game. He drove it up the hill, down the hill and through various obstacles. He even drove it in the water.

Jarrett dreamed of a real red Jeep that he could drive when he was older. He couldn't wait.

One day when Jarrett was eighteen years old, his father called him. "Go to town, son," he said. "Go to the big building that has the words American Electric Power on it. You are going to pay our electric bill. It is very important. They have already sent us three notices. Here is the money – $255. And here is $10 for you. You can buy a toy car if you want. Hurry up, and do not lose the money."

Jarrett was excited. He lived on a farm with his parents, and he loved going to town when he could. It was a thirty-minute walk through the woods.

Jarrett got to town. The first thing he did was go to the drugstore. He knew they sold toy cars there, and he wanted to buy one. But when he walked into the store, he noticed something that hadn't been there before – the state lottery advertisement. "Buy a lottery ticket, and you can win a Jeep," it said. The big prize was a red Jeep. It was exactly the one he had been dreaming of. The second prize was $10,000 and the third prize was $5,000.

Jarrett didn't care about the second or third prize. He wanted to win the Jeep. He didn't buy a toy car. He bought two lottery tickets. Each cost $5. Then he thought about it and bought 51 more tickets. "Fifty-three tickets," he thought. "I must win something." In spite of his father's warnings he had spent all the money his father had given him. Jarrett was eighteen, but his mind sometimes worked like he was still twelve.

The next morning Jarrett woke up because he heard some noise outside. He looked out the window. There was a beautiful red Jeep in the driveway. There were some people standing next to it talking to his father. Jarrett got excited. He ran out of the house. "I won!" he yelled. "I won the Jeep, Dad."

"Are you crazy, son?" his father asked. "These people are from American Electric Power. They have come to cut off the power. You didn't pay the bill, did you?"

Jarrett was so miserable. He confessed everything. His father loved his son. He didn't even get angry. He drove to town and paid the bill himself. Later in the day Jarrett got a phone call from the state lottery.

"Congratulations, sir," a woman's voice said. "You have won $5,000."

Notes

_____

_____

_____

_____

_____

I. Choose the right answer.

1. Jarrett had a huge collection of _____.
   - a. stamps
   - b. toy cars
   - c. butterflies

2. Jarrett dreamed of _____.
   - a. living in a big city
   - b. being an electrician
   - c. having a red jeep

3. Jarrett went to town to _____.
   - a. buy a Jeep
   - b. have fun
   - c. pay an electric bill

4. Jarrett bought _____.
   - a. fifty-three lottery tickets
   - b. two lottery tickets
   - c. a Jeep

5. The men came to _____.
   - a. congratulate Jarrett
   - b. cut off the power
   - c. offer Jarrett a job

6. Jarrett's father _____.
   - a. didn't get angry
   - b. got angry
   - c. was happy

II. **Complete the sentences with the words from the box below.**

drugstore	~~huge~~	various	noticed
warning	confessed	miserable	obstacle

1. Jarrett's collection was very big. It was _huge_____.

2. Something that is difficult to overcome may be called an

   _____.

3. Jarrett used many kinds of obstacles. He used

   _____ obstacles.

4. Jarrett saw immediately that something had changed.

   He _____ it right away.

5. A store that sells medicine, make up, shampoo and

   candy is called a _____.

6. Jarrett's father told him strictly how to behave. He gave

   him a _____.

7. Jarrett felt extremely bad. He felt _____.

8. Jarrett told his father exactly what happened. He

   _____ everything.

III. Choose two words from the box on the previous page and write a short paragraph using them.

_____

_____

_____

_____

IV. Complete the sentences with the expressions from the box below.

dreamed of	care about
cut off	hurry up

1. Jarrett wanted a red Jeep very much. He

   _____ a red Jeep.

2. Jarrett's father told him to move quickly. He told him to

   _____.

3. Jarrett didn't want second or third prize. He didn't

   _____ them.

4. The people came to disconnect the power. They came

   to _____ the power.

V. Choose two expressions from the box above and write a short paragraph using them.

_____

_____

_____

_____

VI. Answer the questions in full sentences.

1. What was Jarrett's favorite toy?
2. What was Jarrett's favorite game?
3. What did he dream of?
4. What did his father tell him to do?
5. What did Jarrett notice at the drugstore?
6. What did he do with the money he had?
7. Why was Jarrett excited in the morning?
8. Why did the men come to Jarrett's house?
9. What did Jarrett win with his lottery ticket?

VII. Oral Summary

Retell the story in a few sentences.

VIII. Written Summary

Write a few sentences to summarize the story.

_____

_____

_____

_____

_____

_____

_____

_____

_____

_____

A TAXI RIDE

I am a taxi driver. It's my job. I can't say that I particularly like my job, but it's OK as long as my passengers don't give me too many headaches. I've been driving a taxi for many years, and I thought I'd lived through it all. A woman hit me once with an umbrella when she couldn't get into my taxi because she was too fat. She said I should think more about average people like her and not only about skinny models. I've had clients with huge dogs and dangerous animals. I've chased cheating husbands and wives. I've been threatened by criminals with knives and guns but survived because I always carry my gun with me. I've played the role of a therapist. I've calmed down people in distress, and once I helped deliver a baby. I thought nothing could surprise me anymore until I met Mr. Humble.

It was about one thirty in the morning. I'd just driven two people to Hotel Seagull, and they had gotten out. I was going to call it a day when a man walked out of the hotel and got into my taxi. The man had been drinking. That was obvious. I've had drunk passengers in my taxi many times before, but this one was different. He was extremely polite.

"Good morning, sir," he said. "My name is Henry Humble, and I need your services. Would you be so kind as to take me to Hotel Seagull, please?"

"But sir," I said. "You are right in front of Hotel Seagull."

"I beg your pardon?" the man said.

"I said that you are in front of Hotel Seagull."

Mr. Humble seemed to be thinking very intensely about something. And then he said, "Could you drive me to Hotel Seagull, please?"

"But sir, you are in front of Hotel Seagull, so I can't possibly drive you there because you are already there."

"Take me to Hotel Seagull," he said. He was getting angry.

I lost my patience. I drove around the block with him and stopped at the same place. "Here you are," I said. "Hotel Seagull. That will be five dollars."

The man gave me a ten-dollar bill. Then he got out and leaned forward to put his head into my window. "Good man, he said. "Keep the change. I just don't understand what the fuss was all about."

Notes

_____

_____

_____

_____

_____

_____

_____

_____

_____

_____

_____

_____

I. Choose the right answer.

1. The taxi driver _____.
   - a. liked his job very much
   - b. thought his job was OK
   - c. hated his job

2. The woman hit him because _____.
   - a. he said something rude to her
   - b. he was driving too fast
   - c. his taxi was too small for her

3. Mr. Henry Humble was _____.
   - a. drunk, and he was being rude
   - b. drunk, but he was being polite
   - c. not drunk, but he was acting crazy

4. It was surprising that the man _____.
   - a. was drunk
   - b. was out after midnight
   - c. wanted to go to Hotel Seagull

5. The taxi was _____ Hotel Seagull.
   - a. in front of
   - b. too far from
   - c. just a five-minute drive from

6. In the end _____.
   - a. both men were satisfied
   - b. both men were angry
   - c. Mr. Humble was very upset

II. Complete the sentences with the words from the box below.

fuss	leaned	threatened	distress
therapist	obvious	intensely	~~cheating~~

1. If somebody is not playing by the rules, we may say he or she is _cheating_____ .

2. A man pointed a gun at the taxi driver. The taxi driver was _____ by the man.

3. A _____ is somebody who could help you through a difficult time in your life.

4. If people are extremely worried and upset, we can say they are in _____ .

5. The man had been drinking. It was clear and easy to notice. It was _____ .

6. The man was thinking very hard about something. He was thinking very _____ .

7. The man bent to be closer to the window. He _____ forward.

8. The man thought the taxi driver was making a _____ about nothing.

III. Choose two words from the box on the previous page and write a short paragraph using them.

_____

_____

_____

_____

IV. Complete the sentences with the expressions from the box below.

call it a day	deliver a baby
gave him headaches	lived through

1. The taxi driver had troubles with some passengers.

    They _____.

2. He thought he had experienced it all. He thought he had

    _____ it all.

3. The taxi driver helped with a birth. He helped

    _____.

4. The taxi driver wanted to stop working that day. He

    wanted to _____.

V. Choose two expressions from the box above and write a short paragraph using them.

_____

_____

_____

_____

VI.   Answer the questions in full sentences.

1. What did the taxi driver think about his job?
2. What kind of clients had he dealt with in the past?
3. What did he think about potential surprises?
4. Who surprised him?
5. How did Mr. Humble act?
6. What did he want?
7. Why was the taxi driver surprised?
8. What did the taxi driver do to get rid of Mr. Humble?
9. How did Mr. Humble thank him?

VII.   Oral Summary

Retell the story in a few sentences.

VIII.   Written Summary

Write a few sentences to summarize the story.

_____

_____

_____

_____

_____

_____

_____

_____

REBORN

Robert Callaghan was at Niagara Falls. He was standing near the railing and looking at the huge waterfall. He was fighting the urge to jump into the water and end his miserable life. His wife had died a few years ago in a boating accident. They had been sailing together when it happened, and he couldn't save her. He blamed himself for her death.

Suddenly he heard a buzzing sound. He turned around. A middle-aged woman was rolling her wheel chair towards the railing. A crowd of tourists made room for her. She stopped her wheelchair, stood up and walked to the railing. Then she climbed over the railing, and in front of the astonished tourists she jumped into the Niagara River.

It took Robert a few seconds to realize what had happened. "She has more courage than I do," he thought. Suddenly he wanted to live only in the moment, so he could save her. He jumped into the river, but he couldn't see her. She had disappeared under the water. Diving used to be Robert's hobby. He took a deep breath, dived in and started to look for her. He found her on his third dive and pulled her to the surface. But now they were too close to the waterfall, and the strong current pulled them towards certain death.

A few minutes ago they had both wanted to die. Now Robert fought for their lives. He put all his effort into the fight, and in the end they were both saved by a rescue team. They were taken to the hospital. The woman was unconscious for three days. When she woke up, Robert was allowed to visit her.

"I know you," she said when she saw him. "I have been dreaming about you. They say you saved my life."

"I'm Robert," he said. "What's your name?"

"I'm Sharon," she said. "You wouldn't have saved me if you knew what I did."

"What did you do?" he asked.

"I killed my husband."

"Did you?" Robert was stunned. "What a coincidence," he thought.

"I crashed into a tree while I was driving with my husband. He was drunk, and he wasn't wearing a seatbelt. My husband was an abusive man. The police thought I did it on purpose, but they couldn't prove it. And maybe I did. That's why I wanted to die."

"I think we have a lot in common," Robert said. "And by saving you, I saved myself. I think we can cope with our sorrow together. What do you say?"

"I would love to," Sharon said and smiled.

Notes

_____

_____

_____

_____

_____

_____

_____

I. Choose the right answer.

1. Robert wanted to _____.
    - a. change his life
    - b. commit suicide
    - c. find a new love

2. Robert wanted to end his life _____.
    - a. because he was ill
    - b. because his wife stopped loving him
    - c. because he felt guilty

3. Robert didn't end his life because _____.
    - a. he was not desperate enough
    - b. he still wanted to do many things
    - c. he didn't have enough courage

4. Sharon jumped into the river _____.
    - a. because she didn't want to live
    - b. because she wanted some attention
    - c. because she was handicapped

5. Sharon suffered because _____.
    - a. she was not able to walk
    - b. she felt guilty
    - c. she had lost her husband

6. In the end they decided _____.
    - a. to deal with their problems together
    - b. to get married
    - c. to find a psychologist

II. Complete the sentences with the words from the box below.

sorrow	abusive	coincidence	unconscious
~~urge~~	surface	current	stunned

1. Robert was so miserable that he fought the
   _urge_____ to end his life.

2. Robert and Sharon were pulled by a strong
   _____ towards the waterfall.

3. Robert found Sharon and pulled her to the

   _____.

4. When they pulled Sharon out of the water, she didn't
   move. She was _____.

5. When Sharon told Robert what she had done, he was
   very surprised. He was _____.

6. Robert and Sharon had similar life stories. Robert
   thought it was a _____.

7. Sharon's husband often hit Sharon. He was an
   _____ man.

8. Robert and Sharon had suffered a lot. They knew what
   great _____ was.

III. Choose two words from the box on the previous page and write a short paragraph using them.

_____

_____

_____

_____

IV. Complete the sentences with the expressions from the box below.

cope with	put all his effort
made room	a lot in common

1. All the tourists stepped aside to let the woman pass.

   They _____ for her.

2. Robert tried really hard to save Sharon's life. He

   _____ into the fight.

3. Robert and Sharon had similar life stories. They had

   _____.

4. Robert suggested that he and Sharon should

   _____ their sorrow together.

V. Choose two expressions from the box above and write a short paragraph using them.

_____

_____

_____

_____

VI.   Answer the questions in full sentences.

1. What urge did Robert fight at Niagara Falls?
2. Why did he want to end his life?
3. What happened right in front of his eyes?
4. What did Robert do?
5. Who saved Robert and the woman?
6. What happened to the woman?
7. Why did she want to commit suicide?
8. What did Robert think about it?
9. What did Robert and Sharon decide to do?

VII.   Oral Summary

Retell the story in a few sentences.

VIII.   Written Summary

Write a few sentences to summarize the story.

_____

_____

_____

_____

_____

_____

_____

_____

_____

THE CHRISTMAS PRESENT

When Jerry Hoffman was just a teenager, he and his friends got the idea to see an old gypsy fortune-teller. They wanted to know who they were going to marry. It was supposed to be fun, but it changed Jerry's life forever.

When the old woman had told everybody about their future wives and husbands, Jerry's turn came. The old woman spread her cards on the table and looked at them for a long time. Suddenly her face became serious and a little bit sad. "Never mind," she said and put the cards away.

"What is it?" Jerry asked. "Come on, tell me. Is she going to be beautiful and rich?"

"I wasn't going to tell you," she said. "But if you insist. You're never going to get married."

"Never?" Jerry was surprised and disappointed. He had not expected that.

"Never unless ..." She paused and looked at her cards again.

"Unless what?" Jerry asked.

"Unless you find the woman fated to be your wife. But it's going to be difficult. I can only give you two hints. I see color and a strange language in the cards."

Jerry wanted to know more, but she refused to tell him. She said she didn't know, but Jerry suspected she did.

Jerry went on with his life, but all his relationships failed. He couldn't forget about the old woman's prophecy. It haunted him.

The years went by, and Jerry was still miserable. He wanted to find the woman who was fated to be his wife, but he didn't know how. He had no idea what the words color and strange language had meant. One day he got an idea. He went to see his friend who was fond of magic and witchcraft. He had read almost everything on the subject.

"I'm not sure," his friend said. "But 'color' might mean she is not white, and 'strange language' might mean she speaks a foreign language. I am sorry I can't help you more."

"She might be anywhere in the world," Jerry sighed. "I'm never going to find her."

Five years later, on Christmas day, Jerry went to the movie theater. There was only him and a woman watching the movie. Jerry felt lonely and invited her for coffee.

"I'm Jerry Hoffman," he said. "And I feel extremely lonely today."

"I'm Dymphna Schwarz," she said. And I feel lonely too." She spoke with a strong accent.

"Strange language," Jerry thought. "But she is white. It can't be her." Then it came to him. "In German 'schwarz' means black! Color! My God, I have found her!"

Notes

_____

_____

_____

_____

_____

_____

_____

I. Choose the right answer.

1. The teenagers had the idea _____.

    a. to see an old gypsy fortune-teller
    b. to play cards
    c. to listen to gypsy music

2. At first the gypsy said Jerry _____.

    a. was going to get married soon
    b. didn't want to get married
    c. was never going to get married

3. Jerry had to find _____.

    a. a woman who was beautiful and rich
    b. the woman fated to be his wife
    c. a woman who would be faithful

4. The hints were _____.

    a. colorful and a strange language
    b. color and a strange language
    c. black and a strange language

5. After asking his friend, Jerry _____.

    a. gave up all hope
    b. began looking in Africa
    c. began looking in Asia

6. Jerry found the woman _____.

    a. in Germany
    b. in Africa
    c. in a movie theater

II. **Complete the sentences with the words from the box below.**

fond	sighed	witchcraft	failed
~~fortune~~	spread	hints	prophecy

1. The old woman predicted the future. She told people their _fortune_____.

2. She put the cards on the table next to each other. She _____ the cards on the table.

3. She told Jerry what she saw in the cards. She gave him two _____.

4. Jerry couldn't find the right woman. All his relationships _____.

5. He couldn't forget about the old woman's _____.

6. Jerry's friend knew almost everything about magic and _____.

7. He liked to read about magic and witchcraft. He was _____ of it.

8. Jerry thought he was not going to find the right woman. He was sad. He _____.

III. **Choose two words from the box on the previous page and write a short paragraph using them.**

_____

_____

_____

_____

IV. **Complete the sentences with the expressions from the box below.**

never mind	fated to be
strong accent	supposed to be

1. The teenagers expected the fortune-telling to be fun. It

   was _____ fun.

2. The gypsy didn't want to continue with her predictions.

   She said, "_____."

3. There was only one woman in the world for Jerry. She

   was _____ his wife.

4. The woman sounded like a foreigner. She spoke with a

   _____.

V. **Choose two expressions from the box above and write a short paragraph using them.**

_____

_____

_____

_____

VI. Answer the questions in full sentences.

1. What idea did the teenagers get?
2. Why did they want to see the old gypsy woman?
3. What did she tell Jerry?
4. What hints did she give him to find his future wife?
5. What was Jerry's life like?
6. What idea did he get?
7. What did his friend tell him?
8. Where did Jerry find the woman he was looking for?
9. How did he know it was her?

VII. Oral Summary

Retell the story in a few sentences.

VIII. Written Summary

Write a few sentences to summarize the story.

_____

_____

_____

_____

_____

_____

_____

_____

_____

_____

FREE AUDIO

You can download a free audio version of the book at

www.easy-reading-esl.com/freedownload8072054.html

NOTES

Printed in Great Britain
by Amazon

76137515R00047